Artwork by: Fammo Gullah of MTAC Inc.
Graphic Design & Layout By:
Inspired Ink Creative Consulting
yogiiw2is@gmail.com

Copyright © 2018 by Lamont Behold
All rights reserved. This book or any portion thereof
may not be reproduced or used in any manner whatsoever
without the express written permission of the publisher
except for the use of brief quotations in a book review.

Closed Eyelids

Part 1

By LaMont BeHold

Contents

Closed Eyelids	3
I'm Not To Blame	14
Back To Self	25
Today I Rain On You	38
Gone Without A Trace	49
The User	51
Broken Sentences	53
Why Change	55
Sheet Metal Music	57
Cry Different	60
I Heard You Singing	62
Stardom	63
Broken	66
Scroll With Me	69
Spot Light For Sixty Seconds	71
Pretty Petals Of Roses	72
It Hurts To Speak	73
Back From Nothing To Something	75
Already Without Life/AWOL	76
Can You Hear My Cry?	78
2 Far From Now/ I Am Not The Man	81
Beautiful Baby (Ain't No Love Lost)	83
Smile	85
The Beauty Of She	86
Self-Contained (Bound 2 Me)	87
Strong But Verbal	89
Can You Relate	93
Free	95

Foreward

We do it everyday, and never think about it..
close our eyes.
In moments of stress or drifting off into rest...the moment we
close our eyelids, we begin to
connect with everything that meets us in the darkness. When
we close our eyes, we exhale and come in to alignment with a
sense of calm that opens all possibility in the darkness.

In "Closed Eyeslids" you will find poetry
strumming the strings to your memory,
picking out pieces you've hidden,
and shining a spotlight on everything that
was, is, and will be.
The words within are written from the heart of a man that
understands the
pain to progress process.
This book will act as a demonstration of the deep desire to
stop long enough to breath life into
the darkness of pain and
PUSH until something happens, and when it does, you'll be
able to open closed eyelids to a bright new day...

Closed Eyelids

Was I ever forgiven

For the sins of all the men she loved

committed

I stare of in a distance

Just wishing that you could visit

I've been crucified by you

Momma

Half way loved on a street level

Tried by you, I've been held afloat at the

moment

And drowned by you

My mind is of you

Momma

Every poem inspired by you

Under these closed eyelids, I ask myself

Lamont, it seems like you were never

forgiven

For all of the sins that were committed

before me

I did just as those men did

I loved and never meant it

They over- saturated her vagina and

planted a broken seed

I cry out for myself

Not ever desiring to be loved by you

I still cry for you Momma

Bruised eye

2 clip wings

Forced out so that I could fly

I still soar for you Momma

My heart roars for you Momma

I began to enable my pain

Soon after your departure

I did just what Momma did

Strangers tried to love me as I hid

Crying in silence

Under closed eyelids

I got to find myself

I stand here

Ready to confront all of my pain and

inflictions

Hey Momma

I still wonder what it would feel like if I

was really loved by you

Hey Momma

I still wonder what it really feels like to be

hugged by you

Momma

My soul has been recaptured

And taking many steps beyond the

confines of your personal rapture

I still look for you Momma

I somehow managed to survive and die at

the same damn time without you

My soul cries out

My steps could never remain stagnant

Today, I'm walking past the abuse

I've been abused by you Momma

I wish I could have said

Don't put your hands on me

Momma

She would beat us until we were bloody

blackened and blue

She would not give our voice permission

She would leave out

Get drunk

Come home mad and in a rage

Throw all of the food out of the kitchen

She would be crying and still delivering

blow after blow after blow

After blow

I would black out and just live in my mind

Now I'm ready to die at the age of seven

Suicidal by the age of eight

Suicidal and depressed by the age of nine

Abuse

Left a dark void inside

How does one defend their selves against

their mother?

I wish I had the strength to say

Don't tread on me Momma

I wish I had the strength to say

Don't take your pain out on me Momma

I wish that I could have said

Don't take that hammer to my head or my

right-hand Momma

Why do you hate me Momma?

Why do you hate us Momma?

Deep in the midst of the abuse

I still cried for you Momma

I'm still surprised by you Momma

Anger and depression constantly sinking

both of our ships

Momma, it's not getting any better

Blank stares

Liquor reaches back to lip

Alcohol and pain were her only two

addictions

I've been beaten black and blue by you

You

The one God sent me to

I'm not ashamed of you Momma

You were not perfect, but you were still

my mother

But Momma

I'm not the blame

I'M NOT TO BLAME

Dear Momma,

Helen

I just can't get over how I was just a child

and constantly being violently abused by

you

I still smile for you

Pardon me for connecting with you

This is half of who I am

The other half

I can't share with you

I got a sickness that I am dealing with

Renewed inside

Renewed my mind

Dear Momma,

Helen

I just can't get over

how I was just a child

constantly being violently abused by you

I still smile for you Momma

And some how

Some way

Through the use of this poetry

I'll make you proud of me, Momma

Now

I'm both lost and found

At the ripen age of 37

Both orphaned and forgotten

By the tender age of 9

Dear Momma,

I still cry for you Momma

She would incautiously beat us in and out

of commission

She would go out and get drunk

Return home

And commence back to her well-known

cycle of abuse

Mental abuse

Verbal abuse

Physical abuse

The type of abuse that no child or adult

should ever go through

Dear Momma

I still cry to you Momma

I cried for you Momma

I'm surprised by you Momma

I'm your gift

Given by the Most High

And I've been denied by you

And declined by you

I grew up self-divided

Abused at age 6

Depressed and suicidal at age 7

No longer wanting to love by the fragile

age of 8

I'm still wishing that I could die by age 9

But I witnessed your death at the age of 9

I witnessed you

Dying

You

Laying besides me

Besides me

Besides

Me

Hey

I still both breathe and achieve for you

Momma

Finally

We are equal

Depression constantly sinking both our

ships

Drinking is how she chose to deal with it

Under closed eyelids

She cried to (WE)

The truth hidden in plain sight

She's drinking again

Putting those liquor spirits to her lips

I've been restrained by you Momma

Mis-ordained and re-arranged by you

Left in a constant hail storm of pain

I still try for you Momma

Liquor and pain was her only 2 addictions

She was beat black by men who she trusted

The true reality of the situation

Here comes the social worker again

Inspecting my bruised blackened body

Reality

My reality

I just keep telling myself

Lamont Behold

Momma was just a little girl that became

over saturated and abbreviated by her

environment

I still live in my head for you Momma

And cry in despair out loud

Under closed eyelids

I wish that I could have said

Please don't tread on me Momma

I'm not the blame for your pain Momma

I wish that I could have said

I love you Momma

I wish that I could have said

Just stop and think Momma

Under these closed eyelids

I am being greeted by pain and reality

I wish that I could have said

Momma

I'm both young and weak

I wish that I could have said

I'm scared and afraid of you Momma

I wish that I could have said

That I can't take no more pain Momma

Under closed eyelids

BACK TO SELF

I just wish that you would die so that you

wouldn't put your hands on me

I still live in my head for you Momma

Dear God,

Was I ever forgiven for all the sins that

were committed before my birth and

before my arrival?

I still cry under closed eyelids

And hell has no furry like a mother who

doesn't know how to love her child

Dear Momma,

The scars that you left behind can be seen

in my physical description

I would be upset and pretend to smile for

you Momma

I would live in my mind for you Momma

Still be kind for you Momma

All because it was you

Who carried me

Under closed eyelids

9 years and 7 months was not enough time

with you

Love comes with both pain and conviction

I stand here

Ever so ready

To greet all of the conflicting convictions

(I ask myself)

Was I ever forgiven for the sins that my

parents created before me?

I open my eyes and gaze off into a distance

I'm halfway whole

And still my heart is missing

How could I ever begin to love you if my

mother never loved me?

I'm getting paranoid again

No longer seeing it fit to ever be drunk out

of my mind

Under closed eyelids

I could never escape my realities

Self-2 Self

Dear self,

Rewind me back 2 free

I am aiming to be greater than you

I am aiming to be brighter than you

I am aiming to be calmer than you

I'm forever aiming to display more

patience than you

Dear self,

I am learning to breathe with you

I am learning to visualize and dream with

you

Dear self,

I just would like to achieve with you

My greatest team is The Most High, I, and

You

Dear self,

I promise to never abandon you

My only option is to make you extremely

better

Self-2 Self

Back to Self

Rewind me back to me

Distance has really served its purpose

My world has collapsed under the frequent

pressure

I still smile while digging amongst the

rubble

Shots have been fired

My soul has been reloaded

Liberation has begun to speak to me

Truth can be heard in any disclosed

location

I've fallen off the grid once more again

Finally

My brother has begun to smile

His essence somehow reminds me of his

father

Finally

My sister has begun to smile

Her essence reminds me of my mother

This is my open letter to humanity

Patience has diligently created a fort

amongst the midst of my storm

The winds keep me calm because they

know that I am in tuned with thee

The storm raging within begins to speak

quietly

The rain has become the soundtrack that I

need to help organize the chaos

Chaos that has vanished in plain sight

Walls have been knocked down before me

The rubbish around me is now my stepping

stones

I have been swept away by the memories

of today

I am no longer dazed

Come find me in spirit

Come find me silently settled in this

perfect occasion of shared divinity

My poetry has found another way to

resurface

My soul has been repaired

My eyes have been prepared to be carried

over the sea

My vision rotates above my broken axis

My legs have been prepared for this

journey

My will 2 survive is strong

My pain has died willingly

My anger has died willingly

I have been emancipated by way of

positive vibrations

I propel these thoughts forward to offer

you humble options

My race has just begun

I have been deprived for so long by the

false freedoms that you offered me

I've had the proper time to examine the

warrior that's contained within me

I've had time to discover the very side of

me that leads me back to this familiar

location

Mercy has shown her face once again

Humility speaks my name

(BeHold) BeHold

LaMont BeHold

I have been resurrected

Each and every word has been given to reattach

you to divine purpose

This is for WE

This is for US

When your past meets your present, it is a

beautiful thing

The only thing left to re-write is the future

I Am

Mister Liberator

I am the unseen (exe) (1) in control

I AM LaMont BeHold

To truly know me

Is to truly love me

Liberation over everything

Be you

King of Self

Stop looking for a blessing and be a

blessing

We were put here to change lives endlessly

THE VESSEL

Today I rain on you

Today... I rain on you

I

Introduce you to this balanced sunshine

I have been waiting here

Just for you

I have been waiting

For this very moment

Inscriptions of life

Seen through the very eyes of MISTA

Today I rain on you

Promise to never place pain on you

Promise to never be ashamed of you

Orchestrator of words

Cab driver of life

Hallowed and swallowed in pride

Hallowed and swallowed inside

Caught

Conspicuously caught

Rotating in the steering wheel

Of

False perceptions

And

Unhealthy intentions

Quickly

I begin to aspire

Leaking through the very roof

You call your brain

Purposely

To get you wet

Calling my showers near

Today I rain on you

Promise to never place pain on you

Promise to never be ashamed of you

It's sunshine

Shimmering

Showing

Sunshine

Sophisticated

Sunshine

Shaded

Sunshine

Sound

Sunshine

This moment of laughter

This moment of you

This very moment of unwanted rapture

Sad to say it

It's misery in this

Fear trapped in this

But most importantly

It's love in this

Today I rain on you

Place pain on you

Promise to never be ashamed of you

Scattering myself into seclusion

Not wanting to be secular

Or submissive

I secrete these tears

Violent tears

These temporary tears

Refreshing tears

Tears of deceit

This being

The moment of imperfect time

Mind being transported to the right place

Eyes focused on these written bit spoken

words

These underlined words

These words of courage

These words of hope

These very words of happiness

These unwanted words of rapture

Hold on tight

I'm still close to you

So, I placed change on you

Today, like no other

We exchange tears

For this very moment we call life

Today I rain on you

Place love on you

I extend myself beyond everything

Just so you can hear

Something with substance

My hands carry my worries

My fears

My loyalty

My responsibility

My strength

My wisdom

Must

I

State

True

Answers?

These uplifting answers

These answers for change

These answers to my questions

These answers to your questions

These answers for the world

You stand still

Here, in a trance

These are my personal answers for life

Today I rain on you

Placed love in you

Today

You are a part of MISTA

GONE WITHOUT A TRACE

Mista
Wealth ain't Wealth
If you have to sell your soul to get it
The world became sick with the vapors
The all-seeing eye continues to rape us
But they replaced us, and my life is stuck in real time
If I'm lost, I can't blame Jacob
Take your time Mista
Hang your head high Mista
Remain in control
Seek self-forgiveness
Life styles lay cemented in an abnormal sense
Functioning to die
Without a trace
Now, we are here
Face to face
My pen ran this race
This may not make sense
Ink all over my face
Gone without a trace
Now, as we sit still
Under closed caption
Holding for a solid commercial break
They sell you out
Your mind is in a lifetime prison
And you can't get bailed out

I'll be standing at the top of the mountain
When it's not raining
But it's raining in my heart
God gave the signs
I digest the Un-digested
Choose not to reject it
Life's broom is too strong
They swept you out of touch
Fighting to hold on
You go and make love to lonely
Now it's only you
Left with no weapon
A product with knowledge
Open for reinspection
I may not be able to save myself
So, I enslave myself
Poetic witness
I ain't never scared
Vocally active
Truth is my reason for living
Ironic scriptures
I'm beauty
Straight from the slave quarters
What do we really stand for?
Nothing
To no thing
Then
GONE

The User

Maybe I wanted to love you
And only you
Please forgive me
I pimped myself away from the realness of her beautiful
content
Fighting with my soul
I got trouble in my mind
I'm fighting to hold on to what is left
Trying not to let go of what was felt
In love
Out of love
In love
And I declined
To be that pimp that pimped himself
We wept
I refused you the third time around
We grew confused
Both in it just for the sex
Beautiful resources
Loving the user was the main reason why you left
I know that loving you could help me understand the
distant parts of myself
This tattered love travelled down
A ridiculous highway that ended nowhere
I remain
Not in love

But above love
Or
Maybe I'm under love
Now needing love
I wish loving you was something that I could afford to do
For the first time, in a long time
I didn't want to use you for my convenience
Please forgive me

BROKEN SENTENCES

The gavel came slamming down the alarm clock of a young
man's life
The judge gave the sentence
His fist handcuffed behind his scared body
He cannot and will not fight
Fell victim to moving that white
The same thing his daddy hustled
Trouble is all that is left
Pain is the only thing felt
He misplaces his guilt
Alone
All he remembers
Is traces from momma's broken crack pipe
The world refuses to understand
His struggle
His life
His hustle
He needs no apologies
His friends aren't around
Just the desolate sound of Satan's voice
FOLLOW ME
His life was the statement in fifteen minutes
His life was changed
Then rearranged
He is standing under an umbrella that can't stop the rain
They call him justice, but he knows none

His life stands still awaiting the verdict
Guilty was screamed loud across the court room
Even Congress heard it
Now, he doesn't have a second chance to dance
He belongs to the State
He couldn't fight for his life today
From the streets
To the cage
And from the cage
To the page
He has become Americas headline
He can't unravel the truth
The sentence became a statement
That statement became this paragraph
Broken sentences require a glue that sometimes The Most
High can't undo

WHY CHANGE

Before I start, let me slow down and peacefully gather myself
I was put here to speak of this life
A life so full of beauty and pain
A life that I will always fight for
This life that Adam and Eve are not the ones to blame
Even though we know the story, we still do the same
Forgive me
I got trouble in my mind and it's not all in vain
I can't afford to wait for change
Some think that the homeless man that lives in the park wants change, but he just wants to change
Trapped inside the cruelness of life
He still gets to witness the lilies when they bloom in the spring
There is possibility even in misery
Like the first cry of a baby when the atmosphere connects with their bodies
Now who got soul?
I really need to know
Born into sin
Born just wanting to glow

My brain became the orchard of my happiness
God bless the Mothers and the Fathers
God bless the Orphans and the Bastards

God
Bless
Me
My young soul speaks of old time knowledge
Life will get technical, and we will not be prepared solely
by the universe
Or
Any type of educational degree
We can't make up for the second time the blood that was
washed away from a sinner's tree

SHEET METAL MUSIC

With my eyes closed and my mind opened, I bring this
I met her on a Thursday
Her worst day
My birthday
Baby's first words
Give me something that I can taste
Who really needs milk when words hide deeply within the
blood of his fragile body
His life began
He takes a look at his only friend
His ears studied her words
Those sweet words that momma use to say

The same sweet words that momma used to say
She would return
In our lost days
Didn't even anticipate
Just like that, momma was taken away
So afraid that I wouldn't listen
Momma was good
Momma was everything
She was living for the wrong reasons
Her life not yet fulfilled, but her lifestyle a little less
honorable to mention
She stuck to this world like grits
Homemade, topped with butter

When things grew thick, she would just hum
The only way she knew how to get through some
unknown song of poverty
I witnessed the music
The sounds use to move swiftly through my heart
Now momma is gone, and I have to keep on
Left alone but not alone
Who would ever imagine that alcohol would tear us apart
Six kids crying for momma
She tried her hardest to play her part
Leaving sheet metal music on a blank sheet for me to
keep

Black Man
You're so intelligent
Wise and sweet
Sweeter than dark chocolate
To: My sisters
Momma said this…
Be a woman
Always be a woman my strawberry queens

Momma used everything in her power to stay music
Made love from broken hugs and daddy's frequent hits
I witnessed her cries of sheet metal music featuring that
bastard on every track

In fact
Momma needed help to touch this ole skin of mine
The flowers on her grave site wait to be watered from my
water
She wasn't perfect, but her flowers sung a song of jazz
A melancholy, today I was a lover, mother, and survivor
kind of song
The song of her life
Recorded on a Thursday
Her worst day
My birthday
And if momma wasn't as good as they said she was, then
why am I still here
Today, I realized that sheet metal music was momma
giving the best of what she had

Cry Different

Forgive me
I'm searching for the right love
Not only at night love
Can't fight love
So, I write love
Invite love in
Forgive me
I'm searching for that over the counter love
The kind of love that loves to love
She didn't believe in love, so she strayed love
Falling in and out of this
Sometimes, I close my eyes and get lost in her soul
For a minute, she said that she loved me, but did she really mean it?
So, now bring it
Sign, seal, and deliver
Sing it
It was a dirty love, so I had to clean it
Bleach it out
I reached out and wiped it out
Now I'm left without the love that I wanted
Baby, I'm giving you permission to floss this because we lost this, and it's been a minute
Sometimes I close my eyes and still get lost in you
I wake up from this dream doubting us
If it was love, then it wouldn't be so hard to see

If it was love, it would just be
I need that warm love
Never cold love
The kind of love that loves to love
That nobody can kill this kind of love
Today, I closed my eyes and got lost in your real love

I Heard You Singing

Dizzy off a Newport…

Please forgive me

Today

I heard you singing

I wanted to sing back

But it was only a memory and I couldn't bring you back

Today

You visited me in words

In prayer

But most of all

In thoughts

I can't explain this explosion that's inside of me

So, I write what's on my mind

Today

I heard you calling for me

For the first time, just like the last time, I couldn't call

back

So, I fall back

Into existence and cradle these thoughts

Thoughts of you

Thoughts for you

Thoughts by you

Today

I saw you looking for me, but I didn't look back

If I could realize what I was looking at

I would feel much calmer when hearing you sing

Stardom

Somewhere
In the cold dry desert, I was left to think
I had to be real swift just to stay alive
Tied up my Jays, and ran really quick to the opposite
direction of the slave quarters…
Nigger Father
Nigger Mother
You a Nigger Lover?
That's how the world said it
I can't regret the color of my skin
It's carrying my soul through this messed up life
May all earth tones remain incognito
Give them their blue, white, and red…Yes, we read it…
They send them away and call it war
We the people must dread it
And if it was about oil, no one said it
Killing our overall innocence
America will never admit it
Gave someone's baby a flag that was laced with gasoline
Satan lit and ran with it
666 are the digits that I don't want for Christmas
I'm thankful to be alive
The long days roll by
And just like you, they all have the will to survive… Or
are they just hanging on just to die?
I arrived

Vote or die

Leave me alone dirty world

This is a real view

When the pain is too overwhelming for their fragility, you lock them away

The truth will not be televised, it is shown

Prison is hell too

Man made laws will isolate and confuse you

Time will not warn a brother

Try to see and hear all

All is connected from the keyboard to the internet

From the jail cells

To the projects

America doesn't trust us to carry ourselves

So, now we worry out of ignorance and burry ourselves

Warning

Crabs are back in the barrel and boiling them won't help

You have been lied to and you don't know why

I lift my hands to the blue stained sky controlling my destiny

God knows I'm in need of a definition

I define myself as being straight, but I'm broken

Broken like two elevens' torn apart

I'm one

One human, one man, one soul, one voice

Hands horizontal

Now grasping the wholesome concept
Somewhere, deep in this forgotten storm
Deep in this well forgotten war
I read, shout, and sing songs of victory
I am the cause
I am the light
A light that shines before and during sunshine
Poetry has me feeling like a celebrity and I ink chase for her sake
A celebrity without restrictions or strange addictions
I'm on an imaginary freeway, destined for greatness…
Until I approach a dead end
Unwind the time
Ask yourself
Are you willing to shine?

Broken

Broken bodies on broken pavements
Can't erase the chalk lines
Lost
Couldn't find their way
Like the masses
Guns spray
Only
For my realest companions to be taken away
All on the same day
We cry
Memories become the face of a thousand kids
Never trying to change this broken future
We lie on our backs
Looking for diamonds in a blackened sky
Accept what has been given
Stop chasing true dreams and never ask why
Broken
This time, fake desires chase my true desires back to hell
No one can tell
I see, speak, and live what they decline to feel
Broken poetry wrapped tightly in God's will
Broken dreams on burnt courts scream the unwanted stories
of the challenged
All things must try to stay dry in this wet environment
Little babies rolling blunts
Babies keep having babies

Getting lifted beyond belief
Open minds on a closed street
Broken
Not a paradise in these heavens…only time for change
Broken boys from broken homes hanging on broken blocks
What you see is not what you get
Getting chased by broken cops sworn to protect you
Breaking bones in the name of justice
God knows because God watches as you get thrown into a broken system
Left to endure being held in his palm
Broken love for a broken promise
That's the breakdown of a production
A broken momma
Thoughts of dismissal for a love long forgotten
Bitter
Rotten
Lost
Baby, you have to love yourself
Can't no man love you like you love yourself
And when it is just you, alone
You will understand
Feeling the rain
Maybe a little too comfortable when the purpose is unknown
Cleansing my soul
Today, I rename the pain

Refreshing
God smiles from the inside of a completed blessing
Broken, but not harmed
Safely yours…

Scroll With Me

Please… Give me back my notebook
I would like to get lost in its words once more
I would forever cherish the fact that the words are
happening right now
I'm in love with this destruction
I'm upset about the equation
Living requires caution
Sometimes, it's a bright red light screaming at you
whenever you look back through that rearview…
It's beauty in hindsight
Victory in the midst of defeat
Smile
You are and will be cherished
I'm praying that the Most High saves us
These blessing will come by DNA
Kings and Queens embodiments
So, I'm praying for your character
Scroll With Me
Third eye blinking
You can't always understand it
You explore the depths
Add a couple of foot and hand prints
Roots need water to grow but apathy will cause the roots
to die

The soul is the treasure, so I detach myself
Toyota Camry's
I figured that I'll just walk this thing out
This thing called life
To be heard is to listen first
Listen and enjoy the friction
Responses should always be positive
Scroll With Me
Come
Grow old with me
Let's enjoy and employ each other
Never destroying one another
Understanding the soul
Lift up and celebrate
We have the victory
Let Us Scroll

Spot Light For Sixty Seconds

You floss so loud
Your style
Loud
I can see fake two miles away
Hidden in-between the seems of your broken dreams
It doesn't fit me well
Can't allow you to lead me to hell
Forget the chains, I want the crown
Forget the name, I cherish my life
These thoughts drift on
How I keep on? It's no mystery
You don't know history
Where is the blue print when we need it?
Let's take the teachers back to school
Change the game up
Sixty seconds of fame up…
I can't blame them
I blame us
The matrix reloads onsite
Men die chasing the spotlight

Pretty Petals Of Roses

A rose froze in blackness
She makes me smile
She creates a sacred place for me to dwell in
She is sweet
She is selfless
She has become my significant Sista
Save me Sista
Set me free
She bears her pretty petals stained with tears
Frozen in between this reckless life and silent death
She was loyal but now she makes me cry
Passing through for the last time
Holding one another in the midst of this lover's light
Loving light
Light of color
Legitimate light of love
Set my soul free
Pretty petals of roses
Allow me to see your roots
Breathe vibrant breath on me

It Hurts To Speak

Don't let America buy you
Be a free agent so they can't sign you
Pastors ain't saying it in the pulpit
I walk alone to find you
Double back the clocks so they can't time you
Unabbreviated justice, I spread this
Not knowing that it is lethal, I send this
Not to be understood, but accepted
Congress can't amend this
My 5th
My rights
The streets will befriend this
Maybe not
Offend this
Composer of realism
My free internal movement
Exchanging Glocks for pens
Tragically, I lost most of my friends
Young boys slaughtered like grown men
Girls interrupted from their innocence
Sex weapons
Babies inhaling the vapors from crack pipes before their throats are developed
My people's minds have been locked away in free wheel chains
Truth disappears
Hope has logically been replaced

The president watches as we lose the race
Claiming to keep us safe
Covering his face like David Blaine
They voted me out
Pre-diagnosed
All for the sake of commerce
Manufactured the so-called remedy, and tried to dope me out
Hoping to pacify my ears, nose and mouth
They re-routed my style as hood
Not to be displayed as good
How can they blame me when they are all up to no good?
Threw my soul into the flames
It's a shame how the people get mislead
The youth will never be exposed to the truth
It Hurts to Speak
If I clone myself, I can be placed between the blue lines on a white
sheet, so when I write and speak, it will sweep the American trash
out of your mind
I'll flood your thoughts to alert you
Far more powerful than this
So, they can't strip siege and search you

Back From Nothing to Something

I had to find myself
Broken words unfold from sealed lips
I was homeless
Helpless
Lonely and hungry
Left naked
Crowned vocalist spreading hope with a pen
Out of breath, running through death
I had to find myself
From nothing to something
Fixing this broken boy so that the man inside can flow
Silence was my only weapon
Light became my only confession
I have found treasure in myself and became lasting ink
Seen the storms of life, I drove in it

Already Without Life/AWOL

Running from my past, I enlisted
I gave up my life-line
Patiently waiting for closure
My fate in the hands of Uncle Sam, there isn't any justice for me
Closed like a flower forced to rot and deprived from its nutrients
Hidden from its water and forced to turn the seeds away
Forever remaining torn from the thresholds of my soil
Roots expected to grow in shallow ground
There wasn't enough love the first time around, so my sunlight has grown into darkness
Against all odds
Death was the only fact
Harsh circumstances, I couldn't hold back
Criminals starting wars to put democracy on the map
Living was no option, but I promised to sing, shout, and stand up solid
Bearing beautiful flowers was my only dream
Closed halfway
Opened halfway
Equally confused, trapped and wanting to see myself again
Reality isn't reality when you're not happy
I'm praying constantly
Steadily
To fulfill these overbearing moments of pain

Even in the midst of my domestic enemies, I will keep joy
here
I brought joy here
The first time around, I couldn't find joy here under any
circumstance
Will I ever give up even if the road begins to close up?
Life begins to hold me up
The sunrise began to show me beautiful things
Reality was the best teacher
The best witness
The best mother
Now, I am caught for going AWOL
Just like a slave being brought back in chains
This is my truth in double feature
The unflattering sides to a man, I ran
My life was in vain
Now I fly with clipped wings to any location

Can You Hear My Cry?

Left dazed and confused, I could no longer hold on to my adjectives
Broken English was accepted
Properly speaking, I have never spoken proper, but my words have life
Words of color come alive
Visions of a million dreams
One hand
One love
One God
So, me and my pen began this cause and movement, but the movement started to move
Trying to catch the bus, running in my Nike tennis shoes
Still couldn't catch up so, they caught us
Locked up
Strapped up
Got Aids on my mind
Got genocide on my mind
I got domestic violence on my mind
Can You Help Me Cry?
Innocent young soul in a new struggle
Old soul in the last battle
Still praying for a better day
Courage fought segregation
Willing to stand together to protect the women and children

Canine's couldn't bite deep enough
Water hoses weren't cold enough
Can You Help Me Cry?
They sell your bright ideas back to you
Pointing their fingers and pistols, asking
"Boy how black are you?'
My body carries my soul, and my soul my blackness
This became my canvas
You spoke without speaking
We never communicated
I wasn't a dread head
Red head
Blonde head
You stopped calling me a nigger
Ignorance set aside
I looked you in your eyes, and told you that it didn't even
matter
It's only a look
Please, stop Brother
We don't even know ourselves
I silenced myself as if I were senseless
My sentence only made enough sense behind the walls of
that jail cell

Every night, redemption came
Locked my body
Can't trap my mind
I don't know why I can't be free
Can You Help Me Cry?
You don't offer me income, but you affirm it
Never showed me any action until the pain ended
Hustling became my tragic reaction
Too strong to cry
My thoughts have awakened to feel the harshness of your thoughts
America
The Beautiful
The Ghetto never fornicated with politics unless she was getting pimped
Behind justice and in front of a million and one faces
Deserving the right to everything
They sell the songs that we used to sing
Crying and relying on faith
Hear Me Cry
Can You?

2 Far from Now/ I Am Not The Man

Braced in between freedom and low expectations, I work for no living
I hunger for my purpose
Ask yourself this. Can you go low as hell?
Nine months on earth without trying to figure things out
There are real things I should know
The things that I would need
The real way to feel, love, and see things with no vision intact
I took my first defecation on this green shrine not knowing the territory
Having no common sense, I declared my ignorance
I Am The Man
I'm suffering just for you
By you
I need you to hold on a little longer
I'm out of touch and feel like I am no longer wanted
My bitter facial expressions describe the story of what use to be and what has left after love became jealous and evolved into dishonest hate
A baby was thrown out the back of a Wells Fargo truck
Wrapped in bills
Doesn't even get a second look
I need you to watch my back and help me spend this

money
My eyes are flooded with doubt
Doubt for the people that I have encountered
Doubting the feeling that never left
Turning my heart away from anything good, beautiful, solid and real
My boots outweighing my limits
Thoughts outweighing my lifestyle, wearing the same bloody white t-shirt
Walking for countless miles
Twenty-three years later, I have come to realize that I haven't traveled far
Only around the corner, and not over the rainbow that constantly flooded my thoughts
Please forgive my run-on sentences
Grieving, standing unconcerned
Noticing the bright light attracting my interest
Chasing me to the middle of the street
Only to realize the cab that has been vacant for the past few minutes is now carrying four passengers…
All of them looking, sounding and acting like me
Should I ride?
I Am Not The Man

Beautiful Baby (Ain't No Love Lost)

No Lost Love
You chose to leave
No return
I've searched for you
I had to learn that nothing last forever
Only these words
You loved but didn't want it back
I resurfaced to find you
Slow these tears down to rewind you
If your love was a song, I would pause it then speed it up
Put the track on repeat just because I couldn't get enough
Now I'm composing and singing all by myself
You're beautiful
You didn't understand what was given
I haven't spoken to you in a long time, but the song deep
inside carries our rhythm
The thought of you keeps me living
Only to die at your hands
It is sad to say, love wasn't in your plans
Now, I'm forced to stand alone
Reminding me of how it felt before you came here
Silent under your conclusion
Beautiful
No love is lost
Reaching out to self

Lover of love, hater of wealth
My soul is rich
All in the name of love
You are beautiful
But you didn't understand what was given
You tried
Our worlds were two of a kind
I'll never speak of this pain
Missing my sunshine
You took my name
I'll never speak of the rain
I promise to grow
Reaching for you forever
Once
In love
You have to be love, see love, give love
Feel love
Reach for it like you never had it
When the truth is found, all things should balance
Beautiful Baby, Ain't No Love Lost

SMILE

Today
I witnessed your beauty from the depths of my soul
Unrehearsed, and not yet sold
Sex sells but not today
Closed caption
I witness you live
Trapped deep within the walls of my heart
It felt good to hold life once again
Perfect timing, I smile for this gift
Uplift and witness this gift from God
Lord Knows
Heaven must be something like you
Heaven must be unheard words born in your name
It can't be forsaken or taken for granted
Truth, it must be
Smile
Close your eyes and realize exactly what this is
Smile
For us
Today I walked out of this sorrowful world and walked into heaven
Today, I found the truth in you
Smile…

The Beauty Of She

She is more beautiful than I could ever imagine
I would appreciate if she didn't mind my infatuation
Love conquers my bruised body
Returning me back to my rare essence
People walk for miles until they are no longer able to bear the love, lies, or the pain
Heartache and distance
On this day
Love was found under no circumstances
She has no unhealthy intentions
She's beautiful not only in my mind, but her love speaks of no pain
Her spirit lingers through this second-hand smoke,
clouding my mysterious memory
Victoria secrets could be found resting on my dark lips
Sweet secrets
God fearing secrets
I get high off her love
So, Let us be
Beautiful to each other
Let us respect each and every factor that will soon determine if this will continue
I shall speak of no other…

Self-Contained (Bound 2 Me)

I build and instill deep black roots anchored in rivers
Representing the ones locked in chains
I am the distant parts of you
Like the fountain that lay flowing on top of a mountain, I move still waters for you
Dividing myself, so that you can listen
We once dreamed a powerful dream
What happened once we arrived?
Wrongly convicted
Face placed in unhealthy locations
Dreaming and speaking alone
Who is the blame for this pain?
I chose not to be affiliated with anything that will hold me bound
Needing to become a better version of me
My spirit won't be conquered
You will not speak against my soul
Depression and pain can no longer fill my mind
I mirror myself to free myself
Breathing easily
I decided to be broke, and went against the American dream
Now, I can't help myself
Placed myself in a position to forget myself
Forging my strengths, I chose to unlock a power that was locked within
I am no longer bound by shallow things that we think make us different
Self-conviction reflection
My thoughts roam around these broken corners
No longer bound by the color of my skin

Eyes lifted beyond the confines of time
Reawakened to impossibilities
Not bound by other people's opinions
Broke free from false desires of the heart
The ego followed, it was holding me
Bound 2 Me
Striving to be
Breathing on purpose
Controlled my thoughts
Affirmed my actions
Reclaimed my cause
Bound… 2 Me

Strong But Verbal

In the middle of the ghetto
My ghetto
Say
Your ghetto
Say
Our ghetto
I assume the position
To be different
Where did it all begin?
Brotha's really got things twisted
Lucifer should never be considered as any type of friend
It's sad to say, but you welcomed him in
You know for a fact that the world is coming close to that realistic end
In the middle of the ghetto
Say my ghetto
Say your ghetto
Say our ghetto
I assume the position
To be different
Spinning loosely on a broken

axis
Some will only fill their
glasses to stand and watch you
from behind
With no class
School is now in session
Not even the dictionary could
define
What man made as their law
Corporate America
The Constitution declines to
support the facts
Statue of Liberty
Victim of domestic violence
Every politician has a gun in
the small of her back
Life and purpose placed
between the broken seams
If you read closely,
intelligence could be seen
In between these lines are half
caged minds
Half stained glass
Running
Away from ourselves
We fall behind first

In all words, the truth will be
heard, but we brag about being
last
So, it will continue to last
You slang it
They blast
You stack it
They count it
Do the math
Man-made sentence
Twenty-five to life
Or 80 percent
Do the math
It happens all over the map
Put here for a reason
So that I can travel down the
hustler's track
Forget selling crack in the
middle of the ghetto
Say ghetto
My ghetto
Your ghetto
Say
Our ghetto
I assume the position to be
different
Showering down crack on
shattered curbs

It's strong
Most importantly
It's verbal
Forgive me as I pay witness
To this murder
Fiends use to be kings and queens
They got lost in their urges
Shhhhhhhh
No one really likes to talk about it
Your brain stays swirling
We ain't strong like the old negroes
P.S
Just things on my mind
Right now, I need a piece of some peace
So that I can rest my mind

Can You Relate

Dazed and used was the
formula they gave me
Now they minimum wage me
Hunt me down and try to cage
me
Throw pistols in my palm
Educationally enslaved me
Outrage me
Exploding in my mind
I suggest every child read
Psalms
It's beautiful music
Trapped beauty in words
Lift every voice and sing
Make a joyful noise unto the
Lord
I sat still
Even though you keep trying
to market my gifts
Constantly raping my very
hard foundation
King me in and out of
extinction
Questions
Real concerns
Real answers
Are y'all really relating?
Questions
Are you concerned about me?
Selling me bull shhh it
Now
Think about it
They say that we are killing
ourselves
And I speak these powerful
words
Orally and casually
With no degree
University of the streets
Life is my teacher
Like I won't fight back
Like I can't fight back

Like I will not fight back
But they just can't figure me out
They won't figure me out
It's God's plan in this man
I won't sink in your sinking sand
The pen just won't leave my hand
Parking my bicycle of life
Leaning on a nine eleven kick stand
I'm surrounded by angels
I done been baptized and filled with the Holy Spirit
Anchored even deeper still
All things are possible
I just won't let the rugged world drown me
Living for the change
Now tell me
Who's thugging?
Who's loving?
Who's a real man?
Who's a real husband?
Who's a real wife?
Who's a real woman?
And if you even care about yourself in the least bit…
Stand up
Breathe
Believe
Recognize the dream
Break the handcuffs
Put your hands up
Achieve
Become what they think they know, but can't see
Become something far more greater
Become
You
Can you relate?

Free

With the Dom still attached
It still doesn't make a thing
free
Free
Dom
Criminals
Decimals
Heroes
And Zeroes
Sent here to spit pro and cons
But who is really the con?
Who is brave enough to blow
that great big horn when the
thickness of the fog hits?
Criminal chasing after
decimals
Changing early future
superstars lives into zeroes
How low will they go to
connect and move that blow
when the thickness of the fog
hits and the realness of it all
hits?

Artwork by: Fammo Gullah of MTAC Inc.
Tyrrellelmore@yahoo.com

The Burden is gone
The exit of it all can also be
Another entrance to pain
If we never learn how to surrender it

It will leave us condensed
Reduced to an afterthought
Of another lesson
Hold Up
Didn't our Grand Mother
before our Mother's Mother
already experience this
so that we didn't have to?

Mental Plantations
Exposing the master within to a symbol
That's how we get caught up
Sold to the highest bidder
Because we have forgotten
What we look like
When we wear ourselves
Contender of a lesser deal

The burden is already gone
We are still collecting energies like
Jordan and Louboutin
As if they're our sparring partners
In this clout battle

Of profitless deals
… Eighty-Six this…
Let's examine freedom

Civil liberties don't always promote self-sufficiency
Once we turn the age of eighteen, we are entitled to self-determination
Determination is the puzzle-piece to aptitude
- A thing used to either enhance, sell or mass-produce our genius -

What are we habitually attracted to?
The view-point is tilted at an angle where
we don't see many fathers in the home…
That one-sidedness is not a creational myth
Our Grand Mothers
Before our Mothers-Mother
Constantly spoke to a man about burdens
How he can take them away

First-hand speculation observed
Where is he?
Pragmatical evidence
When we don't turn on our God from the womb
Our first-sight becomes
Idols of a lesser pact
Hostage of original miracle…

~Anath Sekhem

www.ingramcontent.com/pod-product-compliance
Lightning Source LLC
Chambersburg PA
CBHW081944070426
42450CB00015BA/3340